NETWORK MARKETING

PROFESSIONAL GUIDE IN ONLY 40 PAGES

DR NEO

authorHOUSE®

AuthorHouse™ UK Ltd.
1663 Liberty Drive
Bloomington, IN 47403 USA
www.authorhouse.co.uk
Phone: 0800.197.4150

© 2014 Dr Neo. All rights reserved.

No part of this book may be reproduced, stored
in a retrieval system, or transmitted by any means
without the written permission of the author.

Published by AuthorHouse   03/13/2014

ISBN: 978-1-4969-7509-6 (sc)
ISBN: 978-1-4969-7510-2 (e)

Any people depicted in stock imagery provided by Thinkstock
are models,
and such images are being used for illustrative purposes only.
Certain stock imagery © Thinkstock.

This book is printed on acid-free paper.

Because of the dynamic nature of the Internet, any web
addresses or links contained in this book may have changed
since publication and may no longer be valid. The views
expressed in this work are solely those of the author and do
not necessarily reflect the views of the publisher, and the
publisher hereby disclaims any responsibility for them.

TABLE OF CONTENTS

FOREWORD			01
INTRODUCTION			01
CHAPTER 1			02
CASH FLOW QUADRANT			02
TYPES OF SALE			03
NETWORK MARKETING			04
CHAPTER 2			07
CATEGORIES OF NETWORK MARKETERS			07
8 SKILLS FOR A PROFESSIONAL NETWORK MARKETER			08
PART 1	PREPARATION		09
	SKILL 1	GOALS	09
	SKILL 2	LIST	10
		LIVING LIST HELPFUL TABLE	11
		PROFESSION LIST TABLE	12
PART 2	PROSPECT GUIDANCE		14
	SKILL 3	INVITATION (004)	14
	SKILL 4	PRESENTATION (015)	22
	SKILL 5	EDUCATION AND UNDERSTANDING (016)	23
	SKILL 6	CLOSING (018)	27
PART 3	NEW PARTNER GUIDANCE		28
	SKILL 7	FOLLOW-UP (019)	28
	SKILL 8	PROMOTING EVENTS (020)	30
CHAPTER 3			32
WAYS TO SUCCEED IN LIFE			32
BIBLIOGRAPHY			39
REPORTS			39
ABOUT AUTHOR			40

This book is dedicated to those who took the opportunity to create their own business and do it professionally. I am proud of you, having the courage to follow your dreams.

It is also dedicated to my mentors Jim Rohn, Robert T Kiyosaki and Eric Worre because without them I would not have had the ability and power to help the people in the industry of Network Marketing.

But above all it is dedicated to my wife Barbara who apprehends and motivates me every single day.

FOREWORD

The book you are reading right now was written for my own personal use. It was initially a personal tool I invested in to help myself become a network marketing professional. I then decided to turn into a booklet in which I included all the trainings and seminars I have been to, as well as information from books along with my experiences. The final decision was taken when I read the book 'GO PRO' by Eric Worre.

When I practically saw the difference between a professional and an amateur in me, I decided to turn my notes into a guide, in order to help my team. Then I thought: why not help all the people in the industry of Network Marketing since all of us need guidance? I hope you find it as valuable as it was and it is for me.

INTRODUCTION

I decided to become a Network Marketer for 2 reasons. One was to find time to support my two children and pay off my loans. I realised then that not only could I have more cash flow in my life, but that it also was the only way to reach the status of a millionaire. Through Network Marketing I studied personal development, economics, communication and leadership. The book is constituted in three chapters focusing on three very important issues. The first one stresses the financial issues and the second one is guidance on how to transmute from a simple Network Marketer to a Professional one. The third one describes the five essential educations one should learn in order to achieve anything he/her desires in life.

CHAPTER 1

CASH FLOW QUADRANT

According to multimillionaire specialist in financial education **Robert T Kiyosaki**, there are 4 types of business.

E = **EMPLOYEE**
S = **SELF-EMPLOYED OR SOLO**
B = **BUSINESSMAN**
I = **INVESTOR**

E and **S** are looking for SECURE JOB, though B and I are looking for financial FREEDOM!

E -Have a 'secure job' and feel safe within their comfort zone. They mostly complain about money so they make a living . . . murmuring and waiting for vacations.

S -These people are usually doctors, lawyers, small business owners, accountant who basically work to earn. If they stop working, they simply stop earning. They may have more money than employees but definitely they do not have any time. They make a living . . . working.

B -Someone who has business(es) which somebody else runs for.

I -Someone who makes educated and sophisticated investments.

Both **B** and **I** can make a living . . . living and living . . . giving!

If a Network Marketer acquired professional skills in that industry, he could easily generate **RESIDUAL** income from the **B** quadrant of the **BUSINESSMAN** and thereafter, when having acquired enough education in investments, he/she may also generate **PASSIVE** and **PORTFOLIO** income from the I quadrant of **INVESTOR**.

TYPES OF SALES

TRADITIONAL SALE-Contract involving transfer of the possession and ownership of a good or property, or the entitlement to a service, in exchange for money or value. The commercial transaction involving the sale and purchase of a good, service, or information is called a trade. A trader buys huge amounts of goods in quantities from the manufacturer at a wholesale price and sells it to the consumer at a retail price.

DIRECT SELLING-This is the marketing and selling of products directly to consumers away from a fixed retail location. Forms of direct selling include party plan, one-on-one demonstrations, and other personal contact arrangements as well as internet sales.

NETWORK MARKETING-This is a direct selling method in which independent agents serve as distributors of goods and services, and are encouraged to build and manage their own sales force by recruiting and training other independent agents. By this method, commission is earned on the agent's own sales revenue, as well as on the sales revenue of the sales-force recruited by the agent and his or her recruits called "downline". This is also called multilevel marketing (MLM), cellular marketing, or other names as such. Nowadays it is a multi-billion dollar worldwide industry.

PYRAMID SCHEME-This is an Illegal type of network marketing in which recruits pay an admission fee to join the scheme and earn commissions on persuading other people to join. However little or no product of any real value is exchanged. Such schemes are banned in most countries. These types of schemes have existed for at least a century. Some come with variations in an attempt to hide their true nature. As a result, many people believe that all multilevel marketing plans are also pyramid schemes.

IN **PYRAMID 1** THE PRESIDENT OR OWNER OF ANY CONSTITUTION (BUSINESS, GOVERNMENT, ARMY, or SCHOOL) IS AT THE TOP AND THE EMPLOYEES AT THE BOTTOM. THIS TYPE OF PYRAMID SHAPE COULD BELONG TO TRADITIONAL SALES.

IN **PYRAMID 2**, WE ALWAYS START FROM ZERO AND THEN HOW MUCH WE CAN EXPAND OUR 'PYRAMID' OR ORGANIZATION DEPENDS ON OUR WHYS, SKILLS, PRACTISE AND PASSION. THIS TYPE OF PYRAMID SHAPE COULD BELONG TO THE DIRECT SALES AND NETWORK MARKETING BUSINESS.

NETWORK MARKETING

WHAT REALLY IS NETWORK MARKETING? It is the evolution of franchises like Starbucks, McDonalds, KFC among others, but there are 2 main differences: In a franchise you need an enormous investment and the business itself deals with the local population, while in Network Marketing you can start your business with very low investment and there are no restrictions in regards to who you would like to deal with. It has been proven that the communication method of publicity (mouth to mouth) is much more effective than the traditional one, specifically when the message comes from someone you know and trust rather than from commercial advertisements. Regardless of background, age, sex, colour, education, Network Marketing can give you the possibility and privilege, to achieve enormous success. Of course it all depends on you and your whys, as well as your willingness to learn new skills with passion, patience and persistence.

HOW DOES IT WORK? SIMPLY! First of all you need to become 'one with the product or service'. If you do not believe in it, it is better to move to another company whose product or service fulfils you. Once you realize the benefits, it will be time to help people you know because they will probably need it too. This was the difficult part. Furthermore if you believe in the opportunity then, it is time to help all these people from your organisation. It is however essential that they believe in it too as they will finally have to become independent from you and professional enough to create their own organisation. To achieve the wealth you deserve you will need to commit yourself to working between 5-20 hours per week for 3-5 years.

UNDERSTANDING THE PRODUCT/SERVICE As I mentioned above, after you have tried and appreciated the product, then you are 100% confident that you can present it rightfully and are able to explain what it is, how it works and what the benefits of working with it are.

UNDERSTANDING THE COMPENSATION PLAN Compensation plans vary from company to company. As a general rule, a pay-out of more than 60% indicates that the product/service is grossly overpriced, unless it is unique or exclusively patented. Otherwise it will someday cease to exist just like a pyramid scheme would. Most compensation plans fall into binary, matrix and the previous stair-steps / breakaway and uni-level.

HOW TO START IMMIDIATELY Success will come after two phases have been completed. The 1st phase is to professionally invite and present the idea to as many people you know. The 2nd phase is training the contributors of your team to do the same. With the guidance of your sponsor/expert, you should prepare a list of names and begin to call them and present the idea. Identify your goals and read them 2-3 times per day, to know where you are heading to.

WHY MOST PEOPLE FAIL

There is no passion for learning.
There is no action and if there is, it is not the right one.
There are is no specific goal to achieve.
Excuses about why there are no results.
Compares himself to others.
Quit!

Not taking it professionally and therefore not treating it as a business. Most people say: 'I can think of 5-6 people that could do it! One is my brother, and another is my friend. They both need that product/service. Moreover my uncle who is already a network marketer will love it and my cousin who cannot find a job will definitely go for it . . . . Ok I am IN!!!' Most people hope to recruit some friends and then sit back and wait for the money to roll in. Sometimes they try to convince them but since they are not educated and trained enough themselves they usually end up disappointed, even though they might have been successful at the beginning. Then they blame the system and may even loose friendships.

Robert Kiyosaki focuses on the network marketing industry in his book **The Business School for People Who like Helping People** which he wrote with Sharon L. Lechter. He explains that the 8 values of network marketing industry are:

1. Life changing business education.
2. The value of changing quadrants instead of changing jobs.
3. The value of success into a 'B' quadrant business.
4. The value of investing into the same business the rich invest in.
5. The value of living your dreams.
6. What is the value of network?
7. How your values determine your reality.
8. The value of leadership.

CHAPTER 2

CATEGORIES OF NETWORK MARKETERS

There are 3 kinds of categories in Network Marketing. (001)

1) **IGNORANT** -They will make a list of up to 10 names and feel like they bought a lottery ticket. They hope that by recruiting the first 3-4 key people they will succeed. If the plans do not go as predicted, they either leverage their skill and go to the next category or quit. (See page 5 **WHY MOST PEOPLE FAIL?**)

2) **AMATEUR** -They will make a list of 100 names focusing on luck while hoping to sign the number 1 distributor who will make them rich. The other thing is timing. They feel they want to inform everybody immediately because tomorrow may be too late. They worry about other distributors dominating the local market and the growth curve. They worry about placement in the compensation structure and if they have the right sponsor. They want to place advertisements with their names and telephone numbers all over them hoping that someone will call them.

3) **PROFESSIONAL** -These people will have a living list of more than 1000 people. They will focus on the skills that they will learn from trainings, books, other successful people and their own experience. With the help of their skills, they repeat what they do and get better all the time until there is absolute freedom. PRACTISE->CORRECT->REPEAT->CORRECT . . . .

There are 3 basic rules you need to know in the industry of Network Marketing (NM) (002)

1] You shall be perfect by explaining the products/services of the company you are in.

2] You will know the compensation plan very well.

3] Everybody has the same product/service and compensation plan. YOU are in a line between success and failure. It is up to YOU to succeed.

The financial freedom in the industry on NM can be achieved by you when **YOU HAVE THE ABILITY TO GET A LARGE GROUP OF PEOPLE TO CONSISTENTLY DO A FEW SIMPLE THINGS OVER AN EXTENDED PERIOD OF TIME. THERE ARE 8 SIMPLE ACTIONS** (see page 07).

8 SKILLS FOR A PROFESSIONAL NETWORK MARKETER

- **PART 1** **PREPARATION**
  - **1 GOALS**
  - **2 LIST**
- **PART 2** **PROSPECT GUIDANCE**
  - **3 INVITING**
  - **4 PRESENTATION**
  - **5 EDUCATION AND UNDERSTANDING**
  - **6 CLOSING**
- **PART 3** **GUIDANCE OF NEW PARTNERS**
  - **7 FOLLOW-UP**
  - **8 PROMOTING EVENTS**

PART 1

PREPARATION

SKILL 1

GOALS

WHAT HAPPENS TO YOUR MIND WHEN YOU SET GOALS?

Obviously a lot more than you believe. According to researches by psychologists, psychiatrists, neurologists and other scientists, as well as millionaires, a goal setting is a creation of a plan to achieve something, thinking that you have accomplished it already and reacting accordingly. Obviously the subconscious mind cannot distinguish between the things you want and those you have already accomplished as it does not operate with logic. The subconscious mind will help you to accomplish whatever you ask. In order to succeed in that, you must acquire the skills through your passion, your dreams, and by visualising and feeling it perfectly.

Step by step to Goal Setting.

STEP 1	PAST	What have I succeeded in until now?
		Start the sentence with . . . 'I am proud . . . .'
STEP 2	MISSION STATEMENT	Bear in mind the exact goal, determine exactly what you intend to give in return for the goal you desire, establish a definite date.
		Start with something that describes the picture and feelings.
STEP 3	BENEFITS	Have at least 10 in every goal
STEP 4	COMMITMENTS	Have clear disciplines that must be followed in order to achieve goals.
STEP 5	DAILY PLAN	A routine plan is important
STEP 6	PRAY	To any power you believe in

Achilleas Achilleos B.A.Hyp. (NLP) www.achilleasway.com

Dr Neo

'I will read my goals 2-3 times daily, visualise them and feel them while reading, so they will become one with my subconscious mind. My subconscious mind will thereafter find the way so I can accomplish them.'

What you have is valuable. Nevertheless, the bigger value is not what you posses, but who you become in order to have what you want.

'Why not set a goal to become a millionaire?' **ATTENTION!!!** How grateful would I be if I had $1 million? **No possibility to succeed here.** But if you say . . . 'I have a goal to become a millionaire for what for I will become during the process. I shall do it for what I will end up knowing about the market-place, what I will learn about financial IQ and the management of time and working with people. I will do it to gain the ability of discovering how to keep my ego in check. I will do it to learn about being benevolent and kind, as well as being strong. I will learn about society, business, the government and taxes and become an accomplished person to reach the status of a millionaire. All that I will have learned and all that I will have become to reach the status of a millionaire is what will be valuable. If I do it that way, then once I become a millionaire, I can give all the money away. Why? Because I will already have the skills, and I could do it all again!!!" **(JIM ROHN)**

A way to keep looking at the right direction towards your goals is positive thinking. This can be accomplished through NLP (Neuro-Linguistic Programming) and EFT (Emotional Freedom Technique).

SKILL 2

LIST

    TOOLS: A) **TWO NAME LISTS** in a workbook or in electronic form

                  1) LIVING LIST

                  2) NM (NETWORK MARKETING) LIVING LIST

                  B) Always have a very small workbook or a computer handy for writing notes at any time.

In your LIVING LIST write all the people you know starting with your parents to the last person you can think of.

What's the purpose of doing this list? We live in the information age and regardless of field, your success depends on people you know and keep in contact with. So all you have to do is write down the contact information of every person you know arrange to meet them and find a creative way to stay in touch. It is important to always have this list in case you meet new people. That's why you call it a LIVING LIST. There are no limits on the names on this list.

HOW TO ACHIEVE IT!

1. Use the **LIVING LIST HELPFUL TABLE** (see page 11)
2. Use the **PROFESSION LIST TABLE** (see page 12)
3. Create a goal: add 2-5 new people in the LIVING LIST a week.
4. Socialization: join a gym; find places and organisations to meet new people, get involved in voluntarism, parents associations in schools, create hobbies, join clubs etc.

LIVING LIST HELPFUL TABLE

PARENTS	COUSINS	MOBILE PHONE
BROTHERS	FRIENDS	NETWORK
SISTERS	COMPANIONS*	PARENT'S FRIENDS
GRANDPARENTS	SCHOOL-MATES	RELATIVE'S FRIENDS
UNCLES	COLLEGE-MATES	FRIEND'S FRIENDS
AUNTS	ARMY	OTHERS

* CO-OPERATORS, SUPPLIERS/DEALERS, CUSTOMERS, CONTRIBUTORS, TEAMMATES

EXAMPLE OF A LIVING LIST

NAME	SURNAME	TELEPHONE	EMAIL	OCCUPATION
Neophytos	Neophytou	999999	email@email.com	Family & Pet Doctor

Dr Neo

PROFESSION LIST TABLE

ACROBAT	COACH	FINANCIAL ADVISOR	MANAGER	REFLEXOLOGIST
ACTOR	COFFEEHOUSE KEEPER	FIRE FIGHTER	MANAGING EDITOR	RETAILER
ACUPUNCTURE	COMMISSARY	FISHERMAN	MARTIAL ARTS TEACHER	RHYMER
ADVERTISER/ PROMOTER	COMPOSER	FLORIST	MATHEMATICIAN	SAILOR MAN
ADVISOR	CONTRACTOR	FOOTBALL PLAYER	MEDIUM	SCENARIST
ADVOCATE	COPPER	FOREST RANGER	MICROBIOLOGIST	SCULPTOR
AGENT	CORONER	FORESTER	MIDWIFE	SECRETARY
AGRICULTURIST	COSMETICIAN	FRAMER	MUSICIAN	SHEPHERD
ANALOGIST	CUSTOMS BROKER	GARDENER	NETWORK MARKETER	SHOPKEEPER
APIARIST	DANCER	GEOLOGIST	NEURO-LINQUISTIC PROGRAMMER	SINGER
ARCHAEOLOGIST	DENTIST	GOVERNMENTAL	NURSE / SISTER	SOCIOLOGIST
ARCHITECTURE	DERMATOLOGIST	GRAPHIC ARTIST	NUTRITIONIST	SOUND ENGINEER
AROMATO- THERAPIST	DESIGNER	GREENGROCER	OWNER OF KIOSK	SPONGER
ASTROLOGIST	DETAIL MAN	GUARD	PAINTER	STATIONMASTER
ASTRONAUT	DETECTIVE	GUNSMITH	PAINTER	STENOGRAPHER
ATHLETE	DIETICIAN	GYMNAST- TRAINER	PARK MAN	STOCKBREEDER
AUDITOR	DIPLOMATIST	HANDYMAN	PAWNBROKER	TAILOR
BAKER	DOCTOR	HISTORIAN	PHARMACIST	TEACHER
BARMAN	DRILL MAN	HOMOEOPATHIST	PHILOLOGIST	TECHNICIAN
BASKETBALL PLAYER	DRIVER (TAXI, TRAILER . . .)	HYDRO BIOLOGIST	PHOTO MODEL / MODEL	TECHNOLOGIST
BIOLOGIST	ECOLOGIST	INSPECTOR	PHYSIOTHERAPIST/ KINESIOLOGIST	THEATRE RESEARCHER
BOOKBINDER	ECONOMIST	INSURER	PILOT	THEOLOG
BOTANOLOGIST	EDITOR	INTERNET ADVERTISER	POLICE	TOURIST AGENT
BREAD ROLL SELLER	EDUCATOR	JEWELER	PORTER	TRADER
BROADCASTER	ELECTRICIAN	JOURNALIST	POSTMAN	TRAINER
BROKER	EMBALMER	JUDGE	PRESENTER	TURNER
BUILDER	EMPLOYEE	JUGGLER	PRIEST	VETERINARIAN
BUTCHER / MEAT MAN	ENGINEER	KEEPER	PROSECUTOR	VICTUALLER
CARPENTER	ENTOMOLOGIST	KINDERGARTEN	PSYCHIATRIST	VOLLEYBALL PLAYER
CASHIER	ENTREPRENEUR	LIFEGUARD	PSYCHOLOGIST	WAITER / WAITRESS
CHAMBERER	ESTATE AGENT	LINGUISTICIAN	PYROTECHNIST	WARDER
CHANTER	FARMER	LOCH SMITH	QUARRIER	YOGA TEACHER
CHEMIST	FILM DIRECTOR	LOTTERY	REFEREE	ZOOLOGIST

As in the second list (**NM LIVING LIST**), write down the names you would like to share the information with and be enthusiastic about it. This is a living list as well; each week new names are added on it with the help of your first living list. Bear in mind that for the beginners, this is something new and they may not have the courage to invite people or may not be ready to face rejections. In this case you need to follow a so called beginner strategy.

BEGINNER STRATEGY

In the **NM LIVING LIST** first write down around 70 names of people you **believe*** will not be interested at all. After that write down some names of people you **believe*** will do it for sure. In that way you have just created 2 categories, a **'NOWAY'** category and a **'SURE'** category. When you are ready, start inviting them with the help of your sponsor/expert. By following this strategy, you can eliminate your fear of rejection, get used to it, and become more confident in the future. The reason is that you do not expect them to join the company. Practicing with these 70-80 names will help you get better and reach the status of a professional.

From your guests, you will meet 3 categories of people:
1. The smarty ones who are supposed to know everything.
2. The pessimists who do not believe in themselves.
3. Those who will be enthusiastic and become your partners, or not see again.

By having a better psychological attitude, and a proper invitation and presentation procedure, you may have 3-4 out of 10 joining your company from the **NOWAY** category. That means there is a success of 30-40%.

*I am not the one to judge if the idea is proper or ideal for somebody or not. 'Do I benefit from the product/service?' If yes, then I will let everyone know about it and let them be responsible for themselves to decide if they want to join or not. My job is to educate and make them understand it.

The point of this technique is just to help the beginners to learn, become fearless of rejections and get used to making invitations.

Dr Neo

EXAMPLE OF A NM LIVING LIST

NAME	SURNAME	TELEPHONE	INVITE	EXPOSE	
Neophytos	Neophytou	999999	20/10/13	22/10/13	√

PART 2

PROSPECT GUIDANCE

SKILL 3

INVITATION (004)

Iinviting somebody in a professional way will earn you their respect and it will be hard for them to refuse your invitation. There are four rules you need to obey to accomplish the proper invitation.

RULE 1 You must emotionally detach yourself from the outcome. Just focus on how to make your prospect partner understand it without focusing on signing up a new customer or representative. If the answer is NO, then go to the next one, but keep in touch with the former so they can see your results in the future.

RULE 2 Do not alter your personality when you start inviting people. Be yourself, and at the same time be in your best mood.

RULE 3 Be passionate and don't forget that enthusiasm is contagious. Listen to your favourite music and then make that call. Smile while you talk on the telephone. Clinical researches found that by smiling while having a phone conversation you ensure better communication.

RULE 4 Your attitude will determine your success therefore be confident while you talk on the phone and invite people. You must feel that you don't need them, but rather that you just want to help them.

For the absolute success, you must follow **8** steps so that they say the word **'YES' 4** times.

THE 8 STEPS (005)

STEP 1	BE IN A HURRY
STEP 2	COMPLEMENT
STEP 3	MAKE THE INVITATION
STEP 4	IF I, WOULD YOU?
STEP 5	DETERMINE A DATE
STEP 6	CONFIRMATION
STEP 7	TIME FOR THE NEXT CALL
STEP 8	BE IN A HURRY AND GET OFF THE PHONE OR LEAVE

STEP 1 BE IN A HURRY (006)

Express a feeling of urgency and enthusiasm. People are attracted to those who are busy and happy.

WARM MARKET
1) I don't have the time to talk right now but what I have to say is very important . . .
2) I don't have the time, but it is urgent and I have to tell you now.

COLD MARKET
1) I have to run, but . . .

STEP 2 COMPLIMENT (007)

The sincere compliment will create better communication between you and your prospect as will you change mood into a positive one. This will make the prospect much more agreeable about hearing what you have to say. It is CONFIRMED that this technique works.

WARM MARKET
1) You are very successful and I always admire the way you do business.
2) You've always supported me and I unimaginably appreciate that.
3) You have been the best in what you do ever since I have known you.

	4) I admire your sincerity . . .
	5) I admire your potential character . . .
COLD MARKET	1) You are super sharp and I would like you to be the first to share this important information with
	2) You've given me some of the best services I've ever received . . .

STEP 3 MAKE THE INVITATION (008)

You must acquire the skills to pick out which one of the 3 approaches to use for each of your prospects.

<u>A) DIRECT</u>	How to invite your prospect directly.
WARM MARKET	1) When you told me that you wanted to change your (job, environment, life . . .) were you serious, or just kidding around? **Perfect!** I think I found a way for both of us . . .
	2) I think I found a way for both of us to generate a consecutive cash flow
	3) I found a way for both of us to create a business with minimal cost
	4) If there was a way to replace your full time job with a part-time business, would you be interested in it?
COLD MARKET	1) Have you ever thought about increasing your cash flow? I have something that might be of interest to you.
	2) Do you keep your career options open?
	3) Do you plan on doing what you are doing now, for the rest of your career?
<u>B) INDIRECT</u>	Ask your prospect for help and guidance.
WARM MARKET	1) I've started a business and I need guidance from an experienced mind.

| | 2) | **If the prospect is in another city**: I've started a business and the company has expanded in your area. Would you do me a favour and take a look at it and let me know if you think it would work where you live? |

COLD MARKET 1) I've started a business with a product I think makes a lot of sense. I would like to have your opinion about it. *(I personally use this and it works)*

C) SUPER INDIRECT In other words you should convey to the prospect that they aren't a prospect and that you're just interested in finding out if they know someone who would be interested.

WARM MARKET 1) The business I am in may not be for you, but considering that you understand it, I would like to ask you if you know of any ambitious, money-motivated people who would be excited about the idea of adding more cash flow to their lives?

2) Who do you know that might be looking for a strong business run from home that can benefit them a proliferative residual income?

COLD MARKET 1) The same

STEP 4 IF I, WOULD YOU? (009)

We are offering a value exchange.

If I gave you a CD, DVD, MAGAZINE, would you study it? If I gave you an invitation, would you sacrifice some time and be there?

Very strong question for 2 reasons:
1 They are reciprocal: we say we will do something if they will do something
2 They imply that we have something of value.

One of the three answers are the following.

IF ITS:
YES Then move to STEP 5   **(GOT 1ST 'YES')**
NO Then thank them for their time and leave. DO NOT GIVE THE MATERIAL OR INVITATION, BUT STAY IN CONTACT WITH THEM, SO THEY CAN SEE YOUR RESULTS LATER.

INFORMATION 'I understand you would like more information, but everything you are looking for is on the (DVD, CD, LINK, INVITATION etc). The fastest way for you to really understand it, is to (review the material, come to the seminar). So **if I** give it to you, **would you** (review, come)?'

STEP 5 DETERMINATION OF DAY (010)

When do you think you could . . . . for sure?

Material When do you think you could (watch, listen, read) it for sure?
2 on 1 When do you think it would be cool for you to meet and watch it with a friend of mine who is the most appropriate to analyse it?
Event Would you prefer to meet at a seminar which happens to be this week on . . . . (day), at . . . . (time), to . . . . (place)?

Here the prospect's answer gives us the 2nd 'YES'

In STEP 5 it might be possible to receive an answer such as **'someday I will'**. In this case your reply should be: 'listen, I don't want to waste your time, **NOR MINE**. Why don't we set a real date so we/you could (meet, watch, listen, read it) for sure? We should insist because we already have the '**1**st **YES'**.

STEP 6 CONFIRMATION OF THE DAY (011)

If I called you on . . . . would it be ok?

Assume that the day of the presentation (live, webinar, CD, DVD, link etc) is Tuesday . . . .

Material	Great!!! So if I called you on Wednesday morning, would you have (seen, watched, listened) to it for sure?
Seminar/2on1	Great!!! So if I called for confirmation of our meeting on Tuesday, would it be OK by you?

Here the prospect's answer gives us the 3rd **'YES'**

STEP 7 CONFIRMATION OF THE TIME (012)

Material	We set the appropriate time for calling after the presentation.
Seminar/2on1	We set the appropriate time for calling before the presentation.
Material/Seminar/2on1	'Which would be the most appropriate number and time that I could call you . . . . ?' When attending seminars it is better to accompany your guest there at least 15-20 minutes, before the presentation.

Here the prospect's answer gives us the 4th **'YES'**

STEP 8 I AM IN A HURRY (013)

Perfect! Ok! I have to (run, go)! We will talk then!

More likely 80% will respond!

EXAMPLES: (014)

A) SOMEONE YOU KNOW WHO WANTS TO CHANGE HIS LIFE
DIRECT APPROACH

1. 'Hey, I don't have a lot of time right now but I called you!'
2. 'Listen you've always supported me and I appreciate that! Now it is the time for me to return the favour'
3. 'When you told me that you wanted to change (jobs, environment, life . . .) were you serious, or just kidding around?' **'Perfect!** I think I found a way for both of us . . .'

Dr Neo

4   'If I gave you an invitation, would you sacrifice some time and be there?' (1ST **YES**)

5   'When do you think would be cool for you to meet and watch it with a friend of mine who is the most appropriate to give you all the information you need to know?' (2ND **YES**)

6   'Great!!! So if I called to confirm our meeting on . . . . , would it be OK by you?' (3RD **YES**)

7   'Which would be the most appropriate number and time that I could call you?' (4TH **YES**)

8   'Perfect! Ok! I have to (run, go)! We will talk then!'

B) A GOOD FRIEND
INDIRECT APPROACH

1   'Hey, I don't have a lot of time right now but I called you!'

2   'You are very successful and I always admire the way you do business.'

3   'A friend told me the best thing I could do when starting a new business is to have people I respect take a look at it and give me some guidance. Would you be willing to do that for me if I made it simple?'

4   'If I gave you a CD, would you sacrifice some time watch it?' (1ST **YES**)

5   'When do you think would be cool for you to watch it' **assuming is on Tuesday** (2ND **YES**)

6   'Great!!! So if I called you on Wednesday, would you have watched it for sure?' (3RD **YES**)

7   'Which would be the most appropriate number and time that I could call you?' (4TH **YES**)

8   'Perfect! Ok! I have to (run, go)! We will talk then!'

C) A VERY SUCCESSFUL PERSON
SUPER INDIRECT APPROACH

1   'I know you are busy and have a million things to do, but I am glad I caught you'

2   'You are very successful and I always admire the way you do business.'

3. 'I've recently started something new and I'm looking for some sharp people to co-operate with. The business I am in may not be for you, but considering that you understand it, I would like to ask you if you know of any ambitious, money-motivated people who would be excited about the idea of adding more cash flow to their lives?'

4. 'If I gave you an invitation, would you sacrifice some time to be there?' (1ST **YES**)

5. 'When do you think it would be cool for you to meet and watch it with a friend of mine who is the most appropriate to give you all the information you need to know?' (2ND **YES**)

6. 'Great!!! So if I called to confirm our meeting on . . . . , would it be OK by you?' (3RD **YES**)

7. 'Which would be the most appropriate number and time that I could call you?' (4TH **YES**)

8. 'Perfect! Ok! I have to (run, go)! We will talk then!'

D) COLD MARKET
DIRECT APPROACH

1. 'Now isn't the time and I really have to go . . . but . . .'

2. 'You are super sharp and I happen to be looking for some sharp people.'

3. 'Do you plan on doing what you are doing now, for the rest of your career?' 'Perfect! I have something that might be of interest to you.'

4. 'If I gave you an invitation, would you sacrifice some time to be there?' (1ST **YES**)

5. 'When do you think would be cool for you to meet and watch it with a friend of mine who is the most appropriate to give you all the information you need to know?' (2ND **YES**)

6. 'Great!!! So if I called to confirm our meeting on . . . . , would it be OK by you?' (3RD **YES**)

7. 'Which would be the most appropriate number and time that I could call you?' (4TH **YES**)

8. 'Perfect! Ok! I have to (run, go)! We will talk then!'

SKILL 4

PRESENTATION (015)

BEFORE THE PRESENTATION Whether you are a professional or an amateur in the industry of NM, the best thing to do is to have a 3rd party present (a person, material) as the specialist (presenter). The only thing you have to do is to properly inform the 3rd party about your guest. If the 3rd party is a person, then when you meet them simultaneously you should also inform your guest about the specialist. Always arrive properly dressed and early at meetings and don't forget to be yourself. Your role is to be their consultant so in each question they address to you give them another question to think about. You are there purely for them, so the conversation will only be efficient if you actively listen and make questions.

DURING THE PRESENTATION If you are present at the presentation, then all you have to do is remain reserved, not look around and have your mobile phone switched off at all times. You need to stay focused on the subject, no matter how many times you have watched it before. Your guest will copy you. It's human nature.

Isn't it better for me to be the specialist for my guests?
No because of 3 reasons:

- **REASON 1** No matter how excellent you are on the issue, there are questions for which YOUR answers will not be convincing enough.
- **REASON 2** Your guest may respect your personality but is unaware of how capable you are on the issue and they therefore may not take it seriously.
- **REASON 3** There are people that do not like or can't present the idea, but during their career they may become the best network marketers. When you present the idea to your guests without a 3rd party (which you may even do perfectly), most of the times, there is luck of duplication. Sometimes they may even get scared and not become members.

So WHAT do I have to know?
1   Just be perfect at telling your story in 30 seconds.

A) Who you are.
B) Things that did not go well (time, money, communication management)
C) How NM came in your life.
D) Your results or expectations in the future in a part-time business.

2 Your thoughts should be focused on your guest's education, therefore act as a consultant who connects the prospect to tools, events, or other distributors to help them become educated. If the prospect asks a question, just guide them to the answer, but do not present the answer directly.

3 When the time comes, and after you have created your organisation with the assistance of other more experienced distributors and a lot of repetition, you can leverage your qualifications to a presenter.

4 The expansion of your organisation, the effort and assistance of the CEOs of your company as well as your experience will guide you to become a speaker and a trainer to motivate others to succeed as you did.

OK, HOW does a good presentation, look like?

STEP 1 Make them understand the lifestyle benefits they will gain from the idea you offer.

STEP 2 Make them understand that this is only achievable through NM

STEP 3 Describe why this idea best fits your guests.

STEP 4 Describe the product and the opportunity.

STEP 5 Let other distributors tell their story in 30 seconds

STEP 6 Indicate how smart it would be to start as soon as possible.

SKILL 5

EDUCATION AND UNDERSTANDING (016)

A lot of people misunderstand the way by which they should treat their prospects in the industry of NM. They push them to sign up. That's why most of our guests are aloof, or even negative.

What is imperative is to arrange as many appointments as your prospects need for them to understand the subject, trust you and become fearless enough to say 'yes' or 'no'. On average it takes about 4-6 appointments. Automatically you create a better bond between you and them and the possibilities that they will say 'yes' increase after every appointment.

After the presentation, 2 important questions must be addressed by you.

| Question 1: | **RIGHT** | Which one of them did you like best? The product, the opportunity or both of them? (They have to choose only a positive response) |
| | **WRONG** | Did you like it? (Now they can criticize and most often they do it in a negative way—human nature) |

Question 2: On a scale of 1-10, having 1 as zero, where do you see yourself?

ANSWER	ACTION
SCALE 1	'Thank you for your time . . . .' Aim toward your goals, but keep in contact with them.
SCALE 2-8	'How can I help you, to leverage your scale?' *if there is a 3rd party as a specialist, then:*

For any questions, the specialist is there to help no matter if you know the answers pretty well. It is essential that you do not interrupt even if something goes wrong.

SCALE 9-10   Move to CLOSING (SKILL 6)

QUESTIONS-OBJECTIONS (017)

Separated in 2 categories

CATEGORY 1

LIMITING BELIEF IN THEIR ABILITIES

I really don't have the money	I don't have the time
It's not my thing	I am not a salesperson
I don't know a lot of people	I have no experience
I am too old/young	It's not my type

CATEGORY 2

LIMITING BELIEF ABOUT NETWORK MARKETING

Is this NM / Is this one of those things?	Is this a pyramid scheme?
I am not interested in NM	I don't want to bother my friends
The first ones get paid	How much are you making?

The answers you give should come from your or your colleagues' experiences depending on the question. Always be sincere and use the empathy formula Feel/Felt/Found. '**I know** how you **feel, I Felt** . . . . but here is what I **Found**'

Never answer back aggressively or directly to the point, because you have already "knocked them out". Always remember that you are their consultant and your job is to educate them in order for them to understand it and become fearless about their decision.

EXAMPLES:

I don't have the money . . . 'I know how you feel. I had the same feeling when I did not have the money to start a new business. I didn't have money to pay my bills, let alone buy or invest in something else! But when I thought about it, I realized that if I didn't have enough money now, how was I going to change that in the future? I was tired of being left behind and always scrambling. I wanted more out of life so this is what I did. **I found** a way and it was the best decision I have ever made. If you had the money, would you do it in order to change you financial future? (Yes). Do you think you could find a way to make it happen?

I don't have the time . . . 'I know how you feel. I had the same feeling when I did not have the time to start a new business. I didn't even have enough time make a minor change in my life. I worked for 14-17 hours a day and didn't even spend time with my kids, so I exchanged time with money. The funniest part was that not having work meant not having money. I had to work all the time. When I thought about it, I realized that if I didn't have enough time now, how was I going to change that in the future? **I got tired of looking at my children growing up, while I had a job which allowed me no time to spend with them**. Worst of all our financial future still remained uncertain. So do you know what I did? **I found** a way and it was the best decision I have ever made. If you had time, would you do it in order to change you financial future? (Yes). Do you think you could find a way to make it happen?

<u>**Is it a pyramid scheme?**</u> 'Hmm! **Tell me your story! Did you try it out at some point? What happened?** (Let them feel free to speak) then . . . **'What do you think was the reason you didn't have the desirable success?'** After their answer . . . **'Do you think you really gave it a good shot?'** After the answer . . . . **'Do you think NM is the problem? Or could it have been that your timing and education wasn't right at the time?'**

<u>**I do not want to bother my friends**</u> Tell your story or someone else's story, then ask . . . . *'what makes you think you'd be bothering them?'* Don't say anything more until they answer the question. Then . . . *'If you truly believed in the product/service, would you let your friends know about it, so they can let others know about it?'* Then . . . *'If I could show you a way to share it, without making you feel that it comes from a salesperson, would that help you?'*

<u>**How much do you earn?**</u> The answer depends on how long you've been involved. For the beginners . . . **'I am just getting started and I am very excited about my future. If I hadn't made the decision, nothing could possibly change in my life'** If you've been around for a while and have not had the expectable results yet . . . **'I am working part time on this and it will take some time to get the first results. But since then I've learned a lot of things and I will continue learning and investing in myself for my prosperity and wealth. If I hadn't made the decision, nothing could possibly change in my life'** Tell stories of others as well and if it's possible call them on the spot. Then say . . . . **'But the issue here is not me. It is you. The question is how much do YOU want to make?'**

With their permission, go to the next step **(SKILL 6, CLOSING)**, otherwise, set the next appointment within the next few (1-3) days.

SKILL 6

CLOSING (018)

If they are really ready, and have already been educated, and well informed about the idea, you will be able to guide them in the right way so they make the best decision. You will however have to attain the right attitude and learn the 5 questions you will address them with in advance.

Write down the answers.

QUESTION

1. 'Based on what you've learned, if you were to get started with this company on a part-time basis, approximately how much would you need to earn per month in order to make this worth your time?'
2. 'Why do you desire this amount? (GOAL/BENEFITS)
3. 'Approximately how many hours could you commit each week to develop that kind of income?'
4. 'How many months would you work for those hours in order to develop that kind of income?'
5. 'If I could show you the way to achieve the income you desire, are you ready to get started?'

If the amount they desire is not attainable within the time period they wish to set then, as their consultant you should tell them the following.— 'Your expectations could be attainable only if you devote more hours and time than what you demand. If you are willing to change those expectations, we can talk.'

If they are not ready yet, set the next appointment within the next few (1-3) days for repetition.

PART 3

NEW PARTNER GUIDANCE

SKILL 7

FOLLOW-UP (019)

AFTER SIGNING UP

There are 5 dynamic steps you need to learn and follow theoretically and practically. As usually a more experienced distributor will help you at this point, so you can listen and learn.

STEP 1   CONGRATULATIONS

'I am proud of you for taking charge of your life. From now on, things are going to be different for you and your family.'

STEP 2A   THE TRUTH

'Your success in this business is determined by you and not by me. You will be the difference between success and failure. I am here to guide you and help you. I am here to work WITH you but not FOR you.'

STEP 2B   INDEPENDENT

'My job is to help you become independent from me as quickly as possible. Don't you think that's a good goal?'

STEP 2C   DISAPPOINTMENTS

'There will certainly be ups and downs as you build your business. There will be good times and bad times. I'll know that you will have found yourself in a bad phase when you won't call me, or won't show up for meetings, not answer my calls, or make excuses for yourself and so on. When that happens to you just like it happens to everyone, how do you want me to handle it? Do you want me to leave you alone or do you want me to be persistent and remind you why you made this decision in the first place?'

STEP 3   HOW IT WORKS

1) Educate them in more detail on the compensation plan and product/service. Help them get familiar with their site.

2) Provide them with the best materials and documents to start off properly.

3) Help them find their big WHY. (A part of it, has already been done in SKILL 6-CLOSING-question 2)

4) Train them on what really Network Marketing is.

5) Teach them how to make calls and role-play with them.

6) Start making calls with them!

STEP 4   OUR PURPOSE

1) Help them find their first partner as soon as possible.

2) Help them go to the nearest event being held.

3) Help them get their first payment.

STEP 5   NEXT MEETINGS

Arrange the next meetings with their prospects and be present at them. You are the specialist now and they are beginners who may not overcome disappointments. You should arrange meetings with them frequently even if they do not have any prospect. Do it continually and state deadlines because they are now walking on a fine line between success and failure. If they lean towards success it will be easy to continue, but if they lean towards failure it will be easy to quit.

This depends on:

1) How professional their first enrolment will be, but most importantly how quick?

2) Their first payment.

3) Their first meeting with the team and company in general

4) Their first recognition.

5) Friendships with other distributors having similar goals.

SKILL 8

PROMOTING EVENTS (020)

A] THROUGH WEBINARS

B] TOPICAL TO WORLDWIDE MEETINGS OF THE COMPANY

Something magical is happening while getting away from the daily routine and focusing completely on your dreams. It could be a 3-day meeting; or just a weekend, even a day could be enough! The purpose is to regain strength and go back and do what's necessary to move your business forward.

In those meetings, you get to know other distributors who have the same dreams and thoughts. This constitutes to more social evidence. Listen to stories form successful people.

Your goal is to have as many people as possible from your organisation attending those specialized meetings. This will create the so called **momentum** in your organisation. How do you achieve it? Just edify the next meeting and describe stories of people who succeeded after they attended the event in previous years.

In order to succeed in that, first of all, YOU have to attend to it. That is the only way to feel this kind of energy and meet those successful friends.

MATHEMATICS

1ST EVENT	A Hall full event of 1000 people
2ND EVENT	The same event takes place after a year. From those subordinated 1000, only 500 attended plus new ones—but those 500 are making double the money than the whole hall together.
3RD EVENT	The same event takes place a year later. From those subordinated 500, only 250 attended plus some from the 2nd event, plus new ones—but those 250 are making 4 times the money than the whole hall is making together.

STEP BY STEP TO SUCCEED

- **STEP 1**   FIND YOUR WHY! (GOALS) LEARN TO THINK POSITIVE (NLP, EFT).
- **STEP 2**   MAKE YOUR LISTS PROPERLY.
- **STEP 3**   INVITE PROFESSIONALLY.
- **STEP 4**   PRESENTATION:
    1. EDIFY SPEAKER, AUTHOR, SPECIALIST etc
    2. LEARN TO TELL YOUR STORY IN 30 SECONDS
    3. INVITE/CALL FRIEND TO TELL HIS STORY.
- **STEP 5**   EDUCATION AND UNDERSTANDING ARRANGE AS MANY MEETINGS AS POSSIBLE WITH THEM HELP THEM MAKE THE DECISION THAT FITS THEM.
- **STEP 6**   CLOSING. WE ARE THEIR CONSULTANTS AND OUR PURPOSE IS PROFESSIONAL GUIDANCE.
- **STEP 7**   FOLLOW-UP YOUR NEW PARTNERS PROFESSIONALLY GUIDE THEM TO THEIR INDEPENDENCE.
- **STEP 8**   PROFESSIONAL PROMOTION OF THE EVENTS.

CHAPTER 3

WAYS TO SUCCEED IN LIFE

WHAT YOU SHOULD DO

Success is something you attract by the person you become. (*JIM ROHN*).

In order to succeed, academic/professional education is not number one on the list.

In his book 'THINK AND GROW RICH' N*APOLEON HILL* states that the word education is derived from the Latin word 'educo', meaning to educe, to draw out, to develop from within. An educated man is not necessarily, one who has an abundance of general or specialized knowledge. An educated man is one who has so developed the faculties of his mind that he may acquire anything he wants, or its equivalent, without violating the rights of other people, as well as systems.

For the absolute success, you need to get familiar with the **FIVE** types of education:

EDUCATION 1	MENTAL/SPIRITUAL
EDUCATION 2	FINANCIAL
EDUCATION 3	COMMUNICATION
EDUCATION 4	LEADERSHIP
EDUCATION 5	ACADEMIC/PROFESSIONAL

EDUCATION 1 MENTAL/SPIRITUAL

Personal development means generally becoming better as a human being, a parent, a friend, a brother/sister, a son/daughter, a grandparent etc. it also means becoming better as a businessman and having more faith in others.

Thoughts, beliefs, and feelings create our reality so your life largely depends on what you think, believe and feel. In order to change that, you must identify the thoughts, beliefs and feelings that cause bad moods and replace them with other positive ones, which will lead you to what you desire.

Examples from this section.

MENTORS	BOOKS, AUDIOVISUALS
NAPOLEON HILL	1) THINK AND GROW RICH
	2) THE LAW OF SUCCESS
	3) THE 17 PRINCIPLES OF PERSONAL ACHIEVEMENT
WALLACE WATTLES	1) THE SCIENCE OF GETTING RICH
	2) THE SCIENCE OF BEING WELL
WILLIAM CLEMENT STONE	1) SUCCESS THROUGH A POSITIVE MENTAL ATTITUDE
DALE CARNEGIE	1) HOW TO STOP WORRYING AND START LIVING
	2) HOW TO ENJOY YOUR LIFE AND YOUR JOB
JIM ROHN	1) 7 STRATEGIES TO WEALTH AND HAPPINESS
	2) THE ART OF EXCEPTIONAL LIVING
	3) THE FIVE MAJOR PIECES TO THE LIFE PUZZLE
	4) MY PHILOSOPHY ABOUT SUCCESSFUL LIVING
	5) 12 PILLARS OF SUCCESS
	6) CHALLENGE TO SUCCEED

Dr Neo

ZIG ZIGLAR	1) BETTER THAN GOOD
	2) CONVERSATIONS WITH MY DOG
BOB PROCTOR	1) YOU WERE BORN RICH
	2) STOP WISHING START WINNING
	3) THE GOAL ACHIEVER
	4) IT'S NOT ABOUT THE MONEY
	5) SET FOR LIFE
ANTHONY ROBBINS	1) UNLEASH THE POWER WITHIN
	2) AWAKEN THE GIANT WITHIN
	3) UNLIMITED POWER
BRIAN TRACY	1) MAXIMUM ACHIEVEMENT
	2) EAT THAT FROG
HARVEY MACKAY	1) SWIM WITH THE SHARKS WITHOUT BEING EATEN ALIVE
	2) DIG YOUR WELL BEFORE YOU'RE THIRSTY
Dr. WAYNE W. DYER	1) THE POWER OF INTENTION
	2) YOUR ERRONEOUS ZONE
	3) WISHES FULFILLED
STEPHEN R COVEY	1) THE 7 HABITS OF HIGHLY EFFECTIVE PEOPLE

EDUCATION 2 FINANCIAL

Training for a higher financial IQ.

Even if you are well educated and have a very good job and salary, every month you may run out of money and get deeper into depth. **WHY?**
ANSWER: Regardless of academic/professional education, your financial IQ is low. That means that even if you make more money, you may still get even deeper into depth. All you need is some financial education.

Financial Intelligence is the ability to solve money problems. Financial IQ is the measurement of how capable you are. It is also important to understand the difference between being wealthy and rich.

It is a combination of knowledge in accounting, economics, marketing and law (taxes).

Examples from this section:

MENTORS	BOOKS, AUDIOVISUALS
ROBERT T. KIYOSAKI	1) RICH DAD POOR DAD
	2) WHY WE WANT YOU TO BE RICH (WITH DONALD TRUMP)
	3) CASH FLOW QUADRANT
	4) RETIRE YOUNG RETIRE RICH
	5) UNFAIR ADVANTAGE
	6) GUIDE TO INVESTING
	7) RICH KID SMART KID
	8) THE BUSINESS OF THE 21st CENTURY
	9) THE BUSINESS SCHOOL FOR PEOPLE WHO LIKE HELPING PEOPLE
KIM KIYOSAKI	1) RICH WOMAN
MIKE MALONEY	1) GUIDE TO INVESTING IN GOLD AND SILVER
GEORGE S CLASON	1) THE RICHEST MAN IN BABYLON

Dr Neo

EDUCATION 3 COMMUNICATION

Communication is the exchange of material and spiritual goods between two or more persons. Human communication was created millions of years ago when people felt how much it was needed for survival. Today communication is a part of our lives. It can be done by gestures, words and letters that can be conceptual, verbal or written, respectively. Knowing how to listen to others, understand them, and behave well towards them will eventually make us successful and happy. Always bear in mind that all of us are equal.

Here you will learn how to relate to the seven major personality types, how to be active listener, how to resolve conflicts and how to influence positively.

Since we live in the informational age, communication is indeed the strongest key to any success.

MENTORS	BOOKS, AUDIOVISUALS
DALE CARNEGIE	1) HOW TO WIN FRIENDS AND INFLUENCE PEOPLE
	2) THE 5 ESSENTIAL PEOPLE SKILLS
	3) TIPS FOR PUBLIC SPEAKING
ALAN PEACE	1) WHY MEN DON'T LISTEN AND WOMEN CAN'T READ MAPS
	2) WHY MEN LIE AND WOMEN CRY
	3) WHY MEN WANT SEX AND WOMEN WANT LOVE
	4) BODY LANGUAGE
PAUL EKMAN	1) UNMASKING THE FACE
	2) TELLING LIES
OG MANDINO	1) THE GREATEST SALESMAN IN THE WORLD
BRIAN TRACY	1) THE PHILOSOPHY OF SELLING
BLAIR SINGER	1) $ALES DOGS

EDUCATION 4 LEADERSHIP

If you understand the difference between a manager and a leader, then you are on the right track. A good manager is not necessarily a good leader and vice versa. However he could of course be both.

A leader has the ability to develop strategic systems and create stages and timetables for the achievement of the final result of the noetic formation (vision). With his leadership abilities, he has the power to guide a team of people, from which he gained trust and diachronic positive impact, to achieve the specific goal, having common benefits.

A leader should have four basic characteristics: 1) A vision so big that he can fit the whole world in. 2) The ability to gain trust with his pure character and the willingness to help everybody. 3) Diachronic positive impact on those he leads. 4) The ability to create other leaders.

MENTORS	BOOKS, AUDIOVISUALS
DALE CARNEGIE	1) LEADERSHIP MASTERY HOW TO CHALLENGE YOUR SELF AND OTHERS TO GREATNESS
	2) THE LEADER IN YOU
JIM ROHN	1) THE 60 MINUTE LEADERSHIP CHALLENGE
	2) 2004 WEEKEND LEADERSHIP EVENT
JOHN C MAXWELL	1) THE 21 IRREFUTABLE LAWS OF LEADERSHIP

EDUCATION 5 ACADEMIC/PROFESSIONAL

Education dates back to the era of art and indicates the teacher's effort to achieve the internal culture of the child, according to the school's expectations and goals. Education is of cultural, valuable and social nature and therefore has an impact on humans and their needs. Academic and/or professional education is the final stage for the complete development of general or specialised knowledge and skill.

According to NETWORK MARKETING:

MENTORS		BOOKS, AUDIOVISUALS
ERIC WORRE	1)	GO PRO
RANDY GAGE	1)	HOW TO BUILD A MULTI LEVEL MONEY MACHINE
ROBERT T. KIYOSAKI	1)	THE BUSINESS OF THE 21st CENTURY
	2)	THE BUSINESS SCHOOL FOR PEOPLE WHO LIKE HELPING PEOPLE
JIM ROHN	1)	BUILDING YOUR NETWORK MARKETING BUSINESS
ZIG ZIGLAR	1)	SECRETS OF CLOSING THE SALE
	2)	NETWORK MARKETING FOR DUMMIES
MARY & WAYNE	1)	MAKE YOUR FIRST MILLION IN CHRISTENSEN NETWORK MARKETING
	2)	BE A NETWORK MARKETING SUPERSTAR
DON FAILLA	1)	THE 45-SECOND PRESENTATION THAT WILL CHANGE YOUR LIFE
TOM SCHREITER	1)	BIG ALL TELLS ALL

BIBLIOGRAPHY

1 CASH FLOW QUADRANT — Robert T Kiyosaki
2 GO PRO — Eric Worre
3 THINK AND GROW RICH — Napoleon Hill
4 NLP — Achilleas Achilleos (B.A.HYP NLP)
5 CHALLENGE TO SUCCEED — Jim Rohn

REPORTS

REPORT NUMBER	BOOK	PAGE
001	2013 Eric Worre, Network Marketing Pro.	21
002	2013 Eric Worre, Network Marketing Pro.	28
003	2013 Eric Worre, Network Marketing Pro.	45
004	2013 Eric Worre, Network Marketing Pro.	31
005	2013 Eric Worre, Network Marketing Pro.	48
006	2013 Eric Worre, Network Marketing Pro.	49
007	2013 Eric Worre, Network Marketing Pro.	50
008	2013 Eric Worre, Network Marketing Pro.	51
009	2013 Eric Worre, Network Marketing Pro.	56
010	2013 Eric Worre, Network Marketing Pro.	59
011	2013 Eric Worre, Network Marketing Pro.	60
012	2013 Eric Worre, Network Marketing Pro.	61
013	2013 Eric Worre, Network Marketing Pro.	62
014	2013 Eric Worre, Network Marketing Pro.	62
015	2013 Eric Worre, Network Marketing Pro.	67
016	2013 Eric Worre, Network Marketing Pro.	77
017	2013 Eric Worre, Network Marketing Pro.	85
018	2013 Eric Worre, Network Marketing Pro.	93
019	2013 Eric Worre, Network Marketing Pro.	101
020	2013 Eric Worre, Network Marketing Pro.	111

ABOUT THE AUTHOR

The author is a family man with a beautiful wife and two lovely daughters. His name is Neophytos Neophytou (**Dr Neo**). He has an MA degree in veterinary medicine and a specialized certificate in small animal surgery. He also has a Naturopathy and Homeopathy diploma. He works as a Family Doctor, Holistic Health Practitioner, for humans and animals. He was born on 15/07/77 in Nicosia, Cyprus. While working, he realised that he only exchanged time with money which meant that at the time he belonged to the *S quadrant*. He got tired of seeing his children growing up, while having a job which allowed him no time to help them in order not to live in mediocrity. That is when he decided to find something smart on a part-time basis, so someday he could control his time and not vice-versa. He soon discovered that the only way to achieve that was through communication with a lot of people. After some research, he realized that the only way to manage that kind of communication is with Network Marketing. In his first two years in the business of Network Marketing, he kept learning, but was still in the *S quadrant*. The reason was that he had not managed to become a professional in this industry until then. After hard work, help from mentors, training sessions, books, experiences and other helpful sources, he learned the 5 essential types of education. He then managed to place himself in the *B quadrant* according to the multimillionaire mentor *Robert* T *Kiyosaki*. Now he managed to decrease his working hours and enjoys his life with his family. Mainly he spends his time on three major occupations: prosperity & 'medicare' of 1) humans 2) animals 3) plants and trees Dr Neo also spends some time with gymnastics, shooting and martial arts.

www.ingramcontent.com/pod-product-compliance
Lightning Source LLC
Chambersburg PA
CBHW021047180526
45163CB00005B/2318